INNER
LIGHT

A Resource Book of Christian Poetry & Prose

By Iain Greenshields

MOORLEY'S Print & Publishing

Publishers of Christian Books ——————— Printers

ISBN 0 86071 343 1

MOORLEY'S Print & Publishing

Publishers of Christian Books ——————— Printers
* Copying & Duplicating * Commercial Stationery *
23 PARK ROAD, ILKESTON, DERBYS., DE7 5DA - ENGLAND

LISTEN

Listen to the trees and the flowers as their colourful
      orchestration is a symphony of God's creative genius.
Listen as the stars form a chorus of illumination to sing
      the praise of their creator.
Listen to the wind as it whistles the gay melody of God's
      fathomless ingenuity.
Listen to the sea as it rolls on unchanging as its God.
Listen to the awesome contentment of a sunset with its
      drama to mark the end of a day, only to rise again.
Listen to a new born baby cry and wonder again at the image
      of God.
Listen, Listen for God.

Listen for a cry from a Cross - *"It is finished"*.
Listen in the depths of eternity for the voice that says
      "I love you".
Listen for those healing words of grace and forgiveness
      that flow so freely to us.
Listen in your darkest hour for the word of eternal hope.
Listen
Don't speak
Don't overwork
Be still and Listen, lest you fail to hear his voice.

THE EAGLE

How I envy the eagle
Soaring high above the earth
A habitation in the unspoiled wilderness
Gliding above the mountains
Soaring in the clear blue sky
Free from the earth below.

What a romantic dream, but far from reality
The eagle is far from relaxed and enjoying the scenery
He is fighting each day for his existence
Each day holds the tension of survival
Each winter threatens to be its last.

There is no place to escape to, but to reality
Only there will I find God
He is reality and in all real things.

THE KINGDOM

Isn't God unique.
Only he could call the *"childish"*
        to become *"childlike"*.

THE REVOLUTION OF LOVE

Love is like a revolution
It overthrows the tyrant of self.
Love is not effeminate
It does not embrace without radical change
Because it is pure.

It opposes impatience
It slays harshness and enthrones kindness
It hates envy
It kills pride, to give birth to humility.

Its words speak sweet words that drown rude speech
It seeks to benefit others and dethrone selfishness
It holds back angry words and hateful revenge
It forgives without regret or recrimination.
Love battles against evil to destroy it
It ponders all truth as beauty to be adorned.

Love protects
It does not bring others down to boost its ego
It is not suspicious because it is perfect and drives
                                                    away fear.
It has vision that hopes for the best
It sees beyond what the eye cannot see
It never gives up
It is not a transient emotion.

Love is eternal
It is a never failing stream of life.

When love comes into our hearts it is like a revolution
It takes up arms to destroy all that is worthless and
                                                    sinful.
Love is not soft
It cannot stand side by side with sin
It will never call a truce
It is not satisfied till its enemies are destroyed
Love never rests.

THE PRISON OF MY MIND

I feel imprisoned within my own mind
Hopelessly trapped
Like a caged animal
I want to know the true nature of things
But I cannot go beyond what is
Beyond what is revealed
The frustration is often unbearable
The infinity of *"what ifs"*.

God has revealed true things to us
But not exhaustively
There are a million questions
But few answers
I am trapped in my humanness.

AS OTHERS SEE IT

How the angels must have danced on that Day
A day of sublime joy
Their Creator bringing galaxies and Universes
                                    into being
They sang together with holy praise that
                              glorious day.

How their hearts must have sunk on that
                              awful day
The Son hanging brutalised on a tree
Something too deep even for them to fathom
They would have flown to his rescue but he
                              did not call.

How my heart ought to be moved by this Cross
God has revealed these deep things to me
My joy should be greater than theirs on that
                              first day
The creation of a universe cannot be compared
              to the forgiveness of a sinner.

THE RIVER

The life of God within us begins, like a stream begins
                                  in the mountain.
The world does not notice it. It does not dwell here.
Only He who is above the mountains sees it all.

To begin with, it is a stream, a mere trickle of water.
It has no fish; little life in it.
Yet it flows, aided by the mountain and the rain.

As it flows down it grows and deepens.
Hardly noticing its strength, depth and width.
It flows in a set direction - to its destiny, the ocean.
It cannot fail to reach its destiny!

As it grows it flows faster.
The nearer it gets to its destiny, the slower it flows
Yet it is deeper and wider and more beautiful than ever.

It flows into the vast Ocean,
Not losing its identity,
But gaining a new, a permanent identity, as part of the
                                  vast, Eternal Ocean.
As the river is, so is the child of God.

THE TRAMP

For years I was like a tramp walking the streets.
I was undernourished; drunk and besotted by the world.
My garments were never washed;
They grew filthier and filthier.

Then I saw a pure light,
It showed me how filthy I was.
The light showed me a way,
A way that led to a Cross.

I stood at the Cross, still in my filthy rags.
I felt strangely warmed.
My rags were taken off and placed on the man on the Cross;
I was clean.

But I was naked.
The man on the Cross gave me his clothes.
I was clothed in love and joy and peace;
In patience, kindness and goodness;
In faithfulness, gentleness and self-control.

Often the clothes he gave me get dirty,
But he always cleans me when I go back to the Cross.

THE CHILD OF GOD - LIKE THE SNOWFLAKE

I watched a snowflake fall to the ground today
It was so tender, so intricate; thoughtfully made.

I thought of the great artistry that designed and made it,
Every artist takes care over every detail in his creation.
He had planned the snowflake before he created it,
He determined its size, its delicacy,
He determined when it should fall,
He planned how quickly it should fall,
He knew where it would fall.

A mere snowflake, once fallen, makes no picture,
All the snowflakes, when fallen into one another make a
                                        beautiful picture,
A picture of Winter peace,
A picture of majesty covering the death on the land.

How wonderfully God plans all of our lives to present his
                        beautiful picture to the universe.

LIFE IN CHRIST

I look at the tree and it reminds me of Him
It is strong and its roots run deep
From the outside it looks lifeless
Inside, it is pulsating with life-giving energy.

I look at the branch and it reminds me of myself
He said *"I am the vine; you are the branches."*
The tree bears life to the branches
Our life grows out of His.

In Springtime the tree begins to bud
The bud is small; hardly noticed by anyone
Out of it grows a lush, green leaf.

In Summer the leaf is beautiful
It is fed by the sun and nourished by the tree
In Autumn the leaf begins to die
Even in death it is beautiful.

The leaf dies but the branch remains
The branch waits for another leaf -
A better and everlasting leaf.

———————

NOT FORGOTTEN

I noticed the daffodils today
They were beginning to wither
Once, they were young, strong and beautiful
Soon they would be dead and forgotten.
What pleasure is there in a withering flower?
Other flowers will take their place
Even they will die and be replaced by others.

Life is like this; this is the frustration of life
When we are young and strong, we are noticed and needed
When we grow old we are discarded for others.

But what of the former vigour and life?
People will always forget but God doesn't
He remembers every detail.

One day he will restore his people
They will be strong and never grow weary
They will be young and never grow old
They will blossom and never fade.

THE PATHWAY

I walked along the path
- there were trees bordering all the way.
It was a walk in the shadows.
There were shafts and glimmers of light
- enough to make the way clear.
When I came to the end of the path, I walked out into
                              the full glory of the sun.
It warmed and renewed every part of me.

Our life is like this.
Our walk is a walk in the shadows.
But God gives us enough light to see the way clearly.
We don't know when the path will end;
We do know that when it does end, we shall walk out
                         into the full glory of the Son.

THE OCEAN

O Lord,

      I feel like a child at the edge of a vast ocean.
      I have been your son now for many years.
      Instead of swimming strongly in your ocean, I
                  paddle like a child at its edge.

      The ocean threatens me when the seas swell and the
                         winds roar.
      I am afraid of its power; it perplexes me.
      Yet that ocean, though sometimes violent and
      powerful is always majestic, alluring, compelling.

      I look at the ocean and see its vastness.
      I go out into it and it never seems to end.
      Yet it is always near, beside me and around me.

      At times it brings calm and peace and reassurance.
      It sparkles in the sunlight; it glistens in the
                         moonlight.

      The ocean of this life is in your hands.
      No matter where I am in it, you are there.

SIN TRAIN

The sin train came pounding down the track of life.
I could not hear or see it as it pounded towards me;
I was blind and deaf.

A man called Jesus saw the danger I was in.
He jumped and pushed me to safety,
But the sin train pounded into him.

———————

A SMILING FACE

Behind the smiling face is a thousand deceptions.
Behind the kind eyes, a heart capable of hate.
We never see the heart, we never know the man.
We only know what we are permitted to see.

But God knows!

We put a face on, we hide our faults and lies, our bad
                                feelings and wicked thoughts.
We hide our hatred, our disdain, our unfaithful thoughts.

But He sees them all!

Every bad thought, every hidden act has been accounted
                                for on Calvary.
The Cross takes my guilt away - my inner, awful sins.

Praise God for Jesus!

———————

THE BABY

The baby was born horribly deformed.
They called it a monster.
It was rejected by its parents;
"If only it had never been born."

But it had feelings too.
It was a real person.

God, in his love, yearned for it.
How incomparably tender his love is.
How all-embracing and gentle is his loving kindness.

LOVE NEVER DIES
(A grief observed.)

Love costs us much pain and grief;
Especially when we lose someone we love.

Our tears flow, our hearts ache.
Why?
Because of love.
Many tears speak of deep love.

As the Song says:
  Love is as strong as death,
  Its jealousy as unyielding as the grave.
  It burns like blazing fire, like a mighty flame.
  Many waters cannot quench love;
  Rivers cannot wash it away.

God will heal the broken heart.
He will comfort our grief.
He will turn our mourning into joy.
His love will never fade or fail.

FACING DEATH

It is a brave man who can face death.
It's a fool who scorns it.

MOUNTAINS

Mountains of unbelief will crumble before a faith that
believes in the power of its Lord.

RAGS TO RICHES

I may die wearing rags
But I'll never die a pauper
That very moment, I'll be crowned a Prince.

FEAR

We need light when we stand alone in the darkness.
Darkness without light is terrifying.

ME? GOD? WHO?

I boast that I know God.
How can I really know God?
I hardly even know myself.

A SONG

I am going to stand upon the earth,
On that glorious day of life;
I am going to live, I am going to love, I am
                                   going to reign.

I will see my Saviour then,
The glorious prince of peace;
He is my Lord, He is my God, He is my King.

There'll be no more sorrow there,
No death, no pain, no hate;
We will love, we will wonder, we will praise.

So believe in him now,
For we know that our redeemer lives;
He's in us, he's our hope and our life.

STOP

STOP
Slow down, think.
You are putting the work of God before God himself.

WAIT.
You'll soon tire
You're losing ground.

ONLY those who,
"Wait upon the Lord
- will renew their strength
- will soar on wings like eagles
- will run and not grow weary
- will walk and not faint."

ALL THINGS NEW

What a picture.
The blue of the sky, beautified by clusters of clouds
The sea, glistening in the sunlight
A clear view of the hills with their intimidating
                                    permanence,
The green of the grass broken only by the orchestrated
                                    colours of the flowers.
If this is a picture of a fallen world -
How beautiful beyond description shall be the New Earth.

TRANSFORMATION

Dear Lord,

You made a beggar a prince.

A PRAYER

Lord,

Give me a heart big enough to love.

GOD'S RICH GRACE

Lord,

You have made what was obscene,
a bride for your Son.
You have made what was ugly and worthless,
a bride beautifully adorned.
You have taken me in all my rags, and say to me,
"How beautiful you are my love."

CONSEQUENCES

I have never felt so helpless in all my life
My wee Kitten was writhing, choking in my hands
There was nothing I could do.

We only had her a few short weeks
She brought us so much pleasure
When all around, people were being vile towards us.

She was so full of fun and affection
She would purr contentedly in my ear

Now she is gone forever.
It's so hard to take in
People will say, *"She was only a kitten"*
But she was made by God
She had become a part of our lives.

Death again.
All because of man's sin.
Always the innocent suffer.

A FRIEND'S DEATH

He just lay there - dead
I felt so helpless
I couldn't speak to him
We couldn't laugh together
I couldn't tell him how much I cared.

I felt so frustrated
It was so awfully final.

We lived for different things
I for Christ, and he for self
Our roads will take us to different destinations.

The awful thing is this - we will never meet again.

WHAT IS LOVE?

What is love?
Can any man understand love?

God is love.
His love is perfect.
It's immense
It's generous.

His love is vast,
It's pure,
It's original,
It's beyond understanding.

We look at the cosmos.
We see it, but we cannot fathom or contain it.

God's love is lavish, unexplainable and immeasurable.
Where is the evidence of this love?
Only in the Cross of Christ.

A BIG HEART

I hate seeing lonely people.
It makes me feel empty and sad.
If only I had a heart big enough to love them all;
To give them the comfort and strength they need.

EPITAPH OF A SINNER

Sin promised me so much;
It promised to satisfy me,
It promised me ultimate delight.
It has destroyed my soul.

THE SAD MAN

I saw this man on a Cross.
He was so disfigured, the lowest of humanity.
He was full of wounds and sores.
He was in great agony, in deep sorrow and pain.

"*Surely he was a wicked man?*", I thought.
Then my eyes were opened.
His wounds and sores, were my wounds and sores.
He had become what I was.
This is too deep for mortals!

MAD RUSH

The birds sing with contentment
The sheep and the cows graze in the fields
Everything in nature is at peace
But man rushes from one crisis to the next
He scarcely stops to see, to look, to understand, to rest
He has no peace with himself, his world, or with his God.

PEACE?

There is such peace here among the dead
Is it only here that we will ever find peace?

MY STONE

What will my gravestone say of my life?
Does it matter anyway?
What will the Lord say of my life?
That's what really matters.

PASSCHENDALE

What a contrast between where he lies and where he fell.
Only 19.
He fell on Passachendale Ridge
One among many thousands
Only a statistic.
Unknown to me; born and died all these years ago.
Yet loved by those who felt the pain of his awful death.
He rests in this quiet place, away from the clamour and
                                    terror of battle.
He was never taken prisoner, but now the grave is his
                                    prison.

BE WARNED

We can never go back.

NO WASTE

My time on earth is short, Lord.
Help me not to waste time.
Let every moment of my waking day be yours,
That I may serve you with all my heart.

SO SHORT!

The life that only yesterday,
was a vibrant reality is now only a memory.

THE KEY

Faith is the key that opens the door to the Kingdom,
Christ is the door.

REJOICING IN DEATH

Today a part of me died.
Not all death is sad.
This death has given me freedom.

It's good to die to self.
This is a death I want to die daily,
So that Christ is formed more perfectly in me.

PAID IN FULL

Calvary is the cheque God wrote
Written with the blood of Jesus
To pay for our sins.

THE MENU

The Bible is a menu
It whets our appetite for the things of God
But, you cannot eat a menu
The meal is Christ, the bread of Life
We must eat and taste for ourselves.

BEWARE

Give the Devil a toe-hold in your life,
and he'll soon have you in a strangle-hold.

ESCAPE!

I smoked a cigarette.
Why?
To ease my mind and body.

I took a drug.
Why?
To help me forget.

I looked to drink.
Why?
To drown many sorrows

I was aggressive.
Why?
To pay back for pain.

I was unfaithful.
Why?
To find outside love.

So much in life is escaping,
Running away from awful reality,
There is often nowhere else to run.

———————

NO GOING BACK!

I could have chosen to be a great man,
                    instead I chose to be a fool.

How my past haunts me
That feeling of shame
That feeling of torture in my conscience
How awful to look back.

I never want to go back
Or speak of my past again
Or glory in false illusions
I must sort out today and look to the future.
Thankyou God for saving this fool.

DREAMS ARE ILLUSIONS

We all dream our dreams
          of how we would like our life to be,
But dreams are an illusion
An escape from reality
Only reality counts
We have the power to change each circumstance
      but dreams will one day be our nightmare.

TENDERNESS

Her eyes sparkled
And won my heart
Her eyes were kind eyes
And restored my soul
Her lips touched mine
And my heart melted
Her arms embraced me
And I felt I belonged
Her ears listened
And my life changed.

IS IT LOVE?

Do you hurt inside, when you hurt me with your words?
If not, is it love?
Do you hurt inside, when you glance a hurtful look?
If not, is it love?
Do you hurt inside, when you pull me down?
If not, is it love?
Do you hurt inside, when you abandon me in my despair
                                        and darkness?
If not, is it love?
Do you hurt inside, when I cry?
If not, is it love?
Do you hurt inside, when I am foolish and fall in
                                        front of you?
If not, is it love?
True love hurts, but true love is hurt.
When Love remains through pain, then it is genuinely
                                        love.

———————

PERFECT LOVE

Lord,
How often I want to give you up!
Why?
Not because of you
You are so perfect and good
So true and full of untouched beauty
Because of me!
I can barely live with myself
- with all my imperfections
How can I live with you
- and all your holy perfections
How often I want to give you up
but your love restrains me
A love that never gives up on me!

———————

BARRIERS

How the human heart longs for tenderness
An arm round our weary shoulder
A caring listener
A hand running through our hair
A pure, sweet embrace
Words of tender, caring, kindness
These things are often far from us
Why?
Because we build barriers to love
Oh to take these barriers down
Oh for an unfeined love to take hold of us
Oh for the selfishness to depart.

LEARN TO GIVE

We all want things out of life
To be loved by someone else
Attention
Happiness
Fulfilment
Wealth
Satisfaction
Security
But we never get them all
- because we seldom give!

MANY SIDES TO LOVE

Love,
Is as powerful as the lion,
It is as strong as the ox
As tender as the butterfly
As radiant as the sunrise
As peaceful as the dove.

LONGINGS

I yearn for my childhood days!
Days of sweet delight,
Days of innocence.

I long to be freed from the agony of
                        responsibility
Of carrying other's burdens
Of the staleness in my own life.

I long for Aunt Mary's sweet nature
Her tender care, her loving heart,
Her interest in me.

Such melancholia sweeps my soul.
Time is my greatest enemy.
With all my heart I want to go back
But I know I never can.

INNER PRISON

How can I ever be free

If my soul is like a prison

- Full of law-breakers!

These law breakers need to be put to death

I have no pity for them

They have no conscience

No feeling for me

They would destroy me if they could

Thanks be to Jesus

He has destroyed their power

And one day he will destroy them completely.

TOO OFTEN

How often we curse our lips for the spite and awful words
But do we say sorry?
No!
Pride keeps our lips full of venom.

How often we do foolish things
But do we learn
Seldom
No sooner has night passed than sin is entertained.

How often we think awful things
But do we show self control?
Hardly ever
That stagnant spring remains unplugged.

Our life is marked out by selfish indulgence
- seldom by godly pursuits.

BEAUTY OF LOVE

All human love is imperfect
But beautiful in its own time.

GOD KNOWS

For weeks I was perplexed as I looked at the garden.
The seeds I had planted were growing;
But which were the eventual flowers, and which the
                                                weeds?
It was difficult to tell.
I could not weed, in case I weeded the real thing.

Yet, in two or three weeks the flowers will bud and
                                                bloom;
The weeds will not!

All things are revealed in God's time.

GOD'S GOODNESS

I feel like Cain
Doomed to wander restlessly through this world.
It feels so empty
In my heart I feel that everything is meaningless.

Yet I know that my sin causes this void; this emptiness.
What can I do?
It all feels cold, so dark, so stale
I feel utter desolation inside myself.

It's hard to understand God.
Who can understand a God who says to me:
"My goodness and love will follow you
- all the days of your life."

I look at myself and feel vile and ashamed.
How could I so easily dishonour such a love?

His goodness and mercy and love is so great
I look to the Cross
It assures me of His acceptance of me!
He will always love me!

How incomparably good God is!

A REQUEST

Lord fill me,

        Not with a high degree of worldly wisdom.
        Not with pride and high self-opinion.
        Not with the praise of men.

        Fill me with the Holy Spirit.
        Fill me with his wisdom and strength.
        Grant me his power, in the work of your Kingdom.

GREAT IS YOUR FAITHFULNESS

Life is so temporary
Is this all that there is?
Everything is meaningless!

Then I looked to God and he gave me hope.
He told me that I was like a traveller on a journey
The body I have is just like a tent
A temporary dwelling.

Like a pilgrim, I journey through the desert
I live in my tent but head for a permanent dwelling.

I am fed daily by 'the Bread of Heaven.'
I am guided by the Light of the Spirit.

The nearer I come to the end of my journey,
The more clearly I see the heavenly dwellings.
They appear so beautiful and desirable.

I want to leave my earthly tent
Often my heart groans because it is homesick
But I shall wait quietly for the salvation of God.

This is not all there is.
There is meaning.
Eternal meaning.

SPIRIT'S POWER

Weeks ago we planted seeds in the garden
We tended the ground carefully
We planted with great care.

After a while, some seeds came up.

Much later, two days of rain came
I looked in the garden, and what a difference!
All of a sudden there were shoots everywhere.

The working of the Holy Spirit is like this.
We plant the seed - the Gospel - in men's hearts.
We witness and pray
We see small signs of life.

Then the Spirit comes and pours himself out
The result is incredible!

We need to do our part and to wait patiently.
Watch for the Holy Spirit to send showers of blessing!

POISON

Sin is poison
It looks sweet and tasty, yet it can destroy us.

Often we hunger after what is sinful
We know that it's wrong; but that does not deter us
We want what we know is bad for us.

Sometimes God allows us just a taste
Not enough to poison us
- just enough to make us sick
- just enough to warn us away from what we thought attractive.

How hard the lessons we need to learn
How often we need to learn them
How great and loving is the patience of God.

COME TO ME!

If my heart is sore and my faith is weak,
If my spirit is wounded and my soul is crushed,
If I am down, dispirited and weary,
Some might be impatient, some might despise or hurt me.

But Jesus! He will be gentle
          He will not break the bruised reed,
          Nor quench the dimly burning flame.

He graciously calls to me,
"Come to me, all you who are weary and burdened, and I will
                                                    rest.
Take my yoke upon you and learn from me, for I am gentle
and humble in heart and you will find rest for your souls.
       For my yoke is easy and my burden is light."

STOP!

        Lord,

            I am confused.

            We are sinful, bad and rebellious.
            We deserve nothing from you.

            But you have said you love us;
            Your love is unique.

            Stop us from destroying ourselves.
            Save us from Hell.

            O God, it is so painful;
            I just cannot understand.

TO LOVE IS.....

To love, is to be tender and gentle.

MULTIDIMENSIONAL LOVE

O, where has my love for him gone?
My heart blows so hot and cold.
I wonder how he can tolerate such fluctations.
Yet, he never changes; his love is always the same.

As Paul said,
*'If only we could grasp how wide and long and deep and high
is the love of Christ.
And to know this love that surpasses knowledge.'*

THE WIND

As I walked, I was deeply conscious of your love for me.
It is as if we were totally alone in the world.
I felt I was the only recipient of your unique love,
I wanted to be there for the rest of my life.

Then, the wind blew through my hair
I realised that the wind blows through everyone's hair
So it is with your love
It is not my exclusive property
Save me from such selfishness
Help me to share your love.

HE'S ALIVE

Jesus is alive!
I've just realised this.

He is not a theological speculation.
He is not an academic exercise.

He is to be worshipped
- loved
- obeyed.

LIKE CHRIST

Lord Jesus,

Help me to be like you
"*Who being the very nature of God did not consider
equality with God something to be grasped, but made
himself nothing, taking the very nature of a servant.*"

I can be so proud and ambitious.
As I go forward, help me to realise my servanthood;
To serve you.
To serve your people.
To be your messenger with the Gospel.

Help us both to die to self.
To know the great honour of serving you.

Humble us to be like you, dear Lord.

GOD'S GLORY

We cannot look at the sun for long,
- we would need protection for our eyes.

We cannot stay in the full blaze of the sun for long,
- our bodies need protection or we would die.

God's glory is like this.
In our sinful bodies, we cannot look upon His glory,
It would destroy us.
He graciously hides his glory, like the sun behind a cloud.
Yet we still see the light.

We need new bodies before we can stand in his glory.
Till then we need to be content with faith.

Faith sees the light,
Though his full glory is temporarily hid from us.

FIRE!

A fire has three purposes
It gives light, heat and energy

The fire of God is in every Christian heart
Yet we can often quench that fire
We need to stir up our hearts and free them from all dross.
Then we will burn as a light in the world,
Then the energy, the power of God will be seen,
Then the heat of God's love will warm hearts.

WITH US - IN US

Walk, as if God walked with you.

Live, as if God lived in you.

TIME

No time is wasted time, when we walk in God's will.

PRAISE

My heart is full of song and praise,
It is cheered by the noblest of themes;
My Lord Jesus loves me.

THE HILL

"Who may live on your holy hill?"
The hill we have to climb is steep
Not for the faint-hearted
When we gaze up to the top of the hill
We are discouraged
We need to climb one step at a time
Before we realise, we are halfway up
We must not give up
He who ascends will conquer.

OCEAN POWER

As I stood at the verge of the great ocean
I was overpowered with awe at the power of the waves
They unleashed themselves uncontrollably on the shore
Such vast, naked power was intimidating and frightening
Yet, God made this ocean
His power must be infinitely greater.

We cannot harness the power of the ocean
But God's power is within us
If only we realised this and allowed his power to be
                                        unleashed in us
How transformed our lives would be.

CLEAR VIEW

At the foot of the hill, only our immediate surroundings
                                        are clear
As we begin to climb, the view gets clearer.
We begin to see as God sees
The higher we climb, the clearer we will see
To stay at the foot of the hill, as many do
Is to remain without vision.

GROWTH

The Lord places the seed of holiness in our hearts;
It is the seed from which the fruit of the Spirit grows.

That seed will only grow to fruitfulness, and we to
                                        holiness;
- as we water the ground of our hearts with prayer
- as we weed out the sins that strangle growth
- as we tend daily to the garden of our hearts.

LOSING TOUCH

Lose touch with God, and we lose touch with reality.

THE TASK

Lord,

I have underestimated my task

When I went out to the garden
The soil needed turned, weeded, and prepared
All this, before any crop or fruit is produced
The grass needed cut, the branches trimmed
So much work to make the garden beautiful and
                                    fruitful.
The labour never ends.

Help me here in Cranhill
Give perseverance, patience and kindness
To finish the work you have given me to do.

SIN!

Sin corrupts!
It makes us feel sick.
It disgusts us and makes us feel unclean.
It ruins our vision of Jesus.

Lord, make me holy.
Help me to fear you, to love you, to live for you.

SAD STONES

This is a place of memories
Graves marked by fine sentiments
People remembered by only a few
Soon forgotten by most.

THE GRAVEYARD

The graveyard is a place at the edge of the town,
Hidden from common view.
All around are various aspects of life
- the sheep in the fields
- the river teeming with its life
- houses, keeping the living
People are living without thought of tomorrow
But this place beckons all the living
But it is placed on the edge of town
To help us forget
To keep the conscience still.

The problems of today that vex us.....
Are only the memories of tomorrow.....
And completely forgotten in this place.

———————

LOOK FORWARD

Death is a tool, used to disrobe us of our mortal bodies
And clothe us in our immortal bodies.

READ THE NOTICE BOARD

The Cross is God's public declaration of man's inability
to save himself.

TRUE PAIN

There is an ache, an emptiness in my soul
My heart has been far from you
I have longed for other things
They brought me emptiness and misery.

Give me a fresh hunger for you.

THE DOOR

Jesus is the door to the Kingdom of Heaven
Are we holding the right key?

A BABY'S DEATH

I watched as the father carried his baby's coffin down the
aisle.
It was so sad.....
My heart was aching - it still is.

Who was responsible for this?
The Book says, *"Death came into the world because of sin"*.
But whose fault is it?
They say it was Adam.

But I would have done exactly what Adam did.
The full horror of it struck me - it was my fault!
I am responsible for the sin of the world;
For the death of the baby.
It is my fault there is death.

Thank God for Jesus' sinless and perfect life!
He reversed the process of sin, of disobedience and death.
He bore the guilt of the world's sin;
- instead of Adam - instead of me.

The sadness, the ache, the pain of death remains,
But the baby had a Saviour.

ONLY TWENTY

She was only 20.
How trivial life seems.
Life only held a speedy death for Jacqueline.
Yet, on her stone is a most meaningful picture
It shouts louder than words.
There is a path with trees lining it
It leads to hills in the distance, where the sun rises
It speaks of a new day
A new day without night; without end
God's eternal Day.

ALL FOOLS

All who lie here were fools
Many were "*fools for the sake of Christ*"
But many were fools because "*in their heart they said there
                                        is no God*".

LOVING MEMORY

"*In Loving Memory.....*"
We are all lovingly remembered in death.....
But shown so little of it in life.

URGENT!

This place of death compels me all the more earnestly to
urgently preach the Gospel of Jesus Christ.

POWER

What does it mean to live a 'powerful' life?
How can we know the glory of God?

Only as we desire with all our heart to know Christ.

Only when we really want to be like Christ.
To serve
The way of suffering
Of humility and meekness
Of grace and truth.

These are the things that bring us glory
This is powerful Christianity.

MY CAT

I looked at Mindy lying beside me.
She is so tender and full of life.
Yet animals die, and that is it!
Their death is such a horrible contradiction.
Their death is the fruit of our sin.
How horribly we have marred God's creation.

GOD HELP US

Life is so sad.
I see people around me;
Their lives are so broken.
What is the point to life?
They do not dare think.

How awful it would be for them -
If they really opened their eyes.

I thought to myself;
If only they knew about Jesus!
If only they would listen!

But who will tell them?
Surely we have failed!
God help us!

STOP ME!

Lord,
Why won't you stop me sinning?

My son,
My grace is sufficient to help you.

A SINCERE CRY

Dear Lord,

"What a wretched man I am"
How often I feel like this.
I am so selfish.
I use people thoughtlessly.

Sometimes I despise myself so much
I just want to cut-off my life
I grieve people; I grieve Jesus.

Help me to kill these sinful thoughts and habits.
Give me a heart that desires only to please you.

MY ENEMY - GOD'S ENEMY

Sin is something in me and a part of me, that hates God.
It always wants to do contrary to God's will.

THE SECRET PLACE

There are secret sins and thoughts inside me.
They would hurt people close to me, if they really knew
them.
But God sees every secret, every thought and wrong desire -
how hurt he must be.

If only we realised this - that he sees and is hurt - we
would not be so quick to sin.

THE FORTRESS

My soul is like a fortress.
Satan had conquered it and made it his own.
He strengthened it with sin and temptation.

Jesus rescued me.
He broke Satan's power and deposed him.
Jesus took up residence in my soul.

Satan and sin still attack me.
Their power is strong and often wounds me,
But Satan is no longer the ruler;
He is outside now.

So long as Christ is here, my walls are safe and impregnable
forever.

A SMILE

A smile can quench a thousand tears.

HE LIFTS ME UP

Like an Eagle on outstretched wings
My heart soars up and up to You in praise
I taste the rare air of your pure love
My spirit is alive again!

THE NAILS AND THE HAMMER

My sins were the nails that pinned him to the tree.
His love for me, the hammer that drove them home.

TRUE LOVE

There's the scent of roses
The early morning dew.
There's the splendour of the sun rise
The glory of its setting.
There's the beauty of a still night
The moon sparkling on the ocean.
There's the infinity of the sky at night
The glow of each star.

But none of these can give me love like you give me
None can fill the lonely heart when you are gone.
They cannot make me laugh or cry
They cannot fill my soul with light, the way you do.

SELF

Within the process of self-assertion
There is the inevitability of self-destruction.

GROW UP!

The Lord said to me
It's time for you to be a man of God
Stop triffling with spiritual things
Stand up and be counted
Never be ashamed of me or my word.

HELP US

People who don't know Jesus go to Hell
How awful, yet true
Give us hearts to weep over this
Give us courage to warn people
Come by your Spirit to change people.

FAITH?

The mystery of faith.

A door stands ajar
Shall I go in?
Dare I go in?

Then a voice, *"Come on in"*
I don't promise you good health or power
Take up the Cross and follow me
Come follow me in faith
Be blessed even when persecuted.

Should I stay out?
Should I go in?
Dare I stay in?

TWO OLD MEN

I met two old men in a dream
They were quite different.

One was cynical and drawn
"Has *life been good to you?*" I said.
"No, I am *disillusioned. I hate life. I hate people.
Take your own life, because it's not worth living.*" he said.

The other man was quite different, though in many respects
                he looked similar to the first man.
He told me of a good life.
There had been bad and hard times.
He trusted God and he showed him a clear way.
God had given him hope, love and life.

But who are these people I wondered.

A voice spoke to me, "*They are both you. The choice is your
                own as to which one you will become.*"

PLATITUDES

Victory! Triumph! Power!

I feel none of these
My soul is like a battlefield
Bitter warfare
So many defeats.

Who has the victory?
Not me!

Christ has won the victory
For me
Hope! The Future! Glory!

But now?
Suffering! Striving! Overcoming!
Failure! Heartbreak! Heartache!
Crucifixion!

Victory? Triumph? Power?
Only in the Resurrection.

A GREAT SURPRISE

God!
How glibly we speak of him and to him.

If we were to penetrate to the heart of God
What would we find?

Love!
Love of the purest, unimaginable kind
Uncontainable love
Mysterious love
Explosure, purifying and terrifying love.

Love exploding in my life
Tender love
Strong love
Demanding love
Restoring love
Rebuking love
Redeeming love.

"Follow me" love.

INNER TORTURE

Sometimes I am tortured by a deep inner despair
A despair that I know because of my dark heart
A despair that says, "How could anyone love someone like
me?"

God knows my heart too well
He knows the depth of my depravity
He sees my hidden depths
That nearly kills me sometimes.

I wrestle to understand my response to God
Is it repentance or self-pity?
Do I really know him?
Have I accepted him?

So much hope everywhere
But so often only uncertainty and despair deep within.

MOORLEY'S

are growing Publishers, adding several new titles to our list each year. We also undertake private publications and commissioned works.

Our range of publications includes: **Books of Verse**
- Devotional Poetry
- Recitations
- **Drama**
- Bible Plays
- Sketches
- Nativity Plays
- Passiontide Plays
- Easter Plays
- Demonstrations
- **Resource Books**
- Assembly Material
- Songs & Musicals
- Children's Addresses
- Prayers & Graces
- Daily Readings
- Books for Speakers
- **Activity Books**
- Quizzes
- Puzzles
- Painting Books
- **Daily Readings**
- **Church Stationery**
- Notice Books
- Cradle Rolls
- Hymn Board Numbers

Please send a S.A.E. (approx 9" x 6") for the current catalogue or consult your local Christian Bookshop who should stock or be able to order our titles.